TREKKING
THE SAHARA DESERT

Sonya Newland

WAYLAND
www.waylandbooks.co.uk

First published in Great Britain in 2016
by Wayland

Copyright © Wayland, 2016

All rights reserved.
ISBN: 978 0 7502 8584 1
10 9 8 7 6 5 4 3 2 1

Wayland
An imprint of
Hachette Children's Group
Part of Hodder & Stoughton
Carmelite House
50 Victoria Embankment
London EC4Y 0DZ

An Hachette UK Company
www.hachette.co.uk

www.hachettechildrens.co.uk

A catalogue for this title is available from
the British Library

Printed and bound in China

Produced for Wayland by
White-Thomson Publishing Ltd
www.wtpub.co.uk

Author: Sonya Newland
Designer: Rocket Design (East Anglia) Ltd
Picture researcher: Izzi Howell
Map: Stefan Chabluk
Wayland editor: Elizabeth Brent

CONTENTS

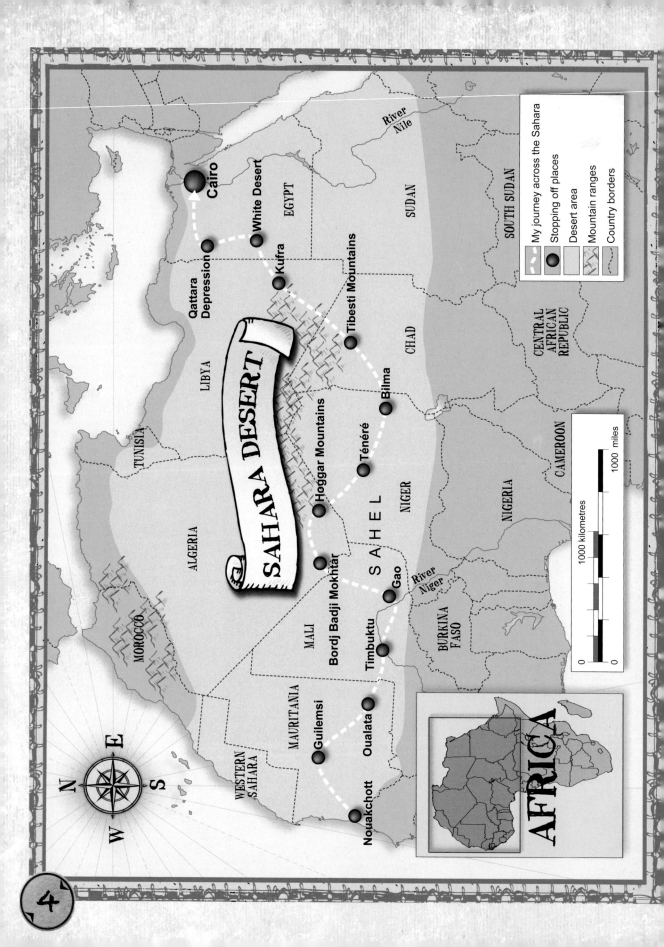

River Nile

SOUTH SUDAN

SUDAN

Cairo

White Desert

EGYPT

Kufra

Qattara Depression

Tibesti Mountains

CENTRAL AFRICAN REPUBLIC

LIBYA

CHAD

Bilma

SAHARA DESERT

Hoggar Mountains

Ténéré

CAMEROON

TUNISIA

S A H E L

NIGER

ALGERIA

NIGERIA

Bordj Badji Mokhtar

Gao

River Niger

BURKINA FASO

MOROCCO

MALI

Timbuktu

WESTERN SAHARA

MAURITANIA

Guilemsi

Oualata

AFRICA

Nouakchott

N E S W

My journey across the Sahara
- Stopping off places
- Desert area
- Mountain ranges
- Country borders

1000 kilometres

1000 miles

1000 miles

0

0

THE SAHARA DESERT

Preparing for the trip

I'm so excited! On 16 October I set off on the journey of a lifetime across the amazing Sahara Desert (see map opposite). These days lots of people explore the Sahara in a four-wheel drive, but I'm starting with a more traditional form of transport – camel! This is one of the harshest landscapes on earth so I'm prepared for some tough going, but I'll have a guide for some of the way and I've been training for months. I'm ready!

At 9 million square km, the Sahara is the largest dry desert in the world. It stretches across the whole of North Africa, from the Atlantic Ocean in the west to the Red Sea in the east. This vast desert blankets parts of 10 countries – Mauritania, Morocco, Algeria, Mali, Niger, Tunisia, Chad, Libya, Sudan and Egypt – and the territory of Western Sahara.

Climate

To survive in the Sahara, timing is everything. In the winter months, the temperature in the desert can drop below freezing at night, and ice can even form. At the height of summer, daytime temperatures can soar to a deadly 40 °C. There's also a higher chance of sandstorms in the spring. Rain is rare in the Sahara – on average there's only about 2.5 cm of rain a year. Some parts of the desert can go without rain for 10 years or more.

Equipment

I've decided to bring along the following:

- hat
- walking boots
- long trousers
- first aid kit
- map and compass
- sun cream
- tent
- torch
- matches
- sunglasses
- binoculars
- sheet of tarpaulin
- signalling mirror
- water bottle
- sleeping bag
- whistle
- strip of muslin

30 October
Nouakchott to Guilemsi

Well, I've certainly learnt a lot in my first couple of weeks in the desert! I met up with my guide – and my camel – in Nouakchott and we headed straight off into the wilderness. We travelled north-eastwards towards the heart of Mauritania because I wanted to see some of the rock paintings here at Guilemsi. This amazing ancient art is proof that people have made their home here in the desert for thousands of years.

Much of Nouakchott's population is nomadic, living there for a while then moving on.

Nouakchott

Mauritania is a country on the western edge of the African continent. Fifty years ago, Nouakchott was little more than a fishing village, but when Mauritania gained independence from France in 1960, Nouakchott was chosen as the new capital. Since then, it has developed into a small but thriving city near the Atlantic Ocean. Droughts have caused many people to move here from surrounding areas, which has contributed to its growth.

Be smart, survive!

The first few days riding a camel were hard work, but my guide gave me some tips to make things easier. Wearing long trousers is essential to stop your legs getting chafed and sunburnt. There are no stirrups on a camel saddle, so don't grip tightly to its sides, let your legs hang loose. Take a break every few hours and walk around so you don't get too stiff. Most importantly - relax and enjoy the ride!

Saharan landscapes

The part of the desert we've been travelling through is sandy, but not all of the Sahara is like this. Huge stretches are made up of bare rock and gravel. There are also high ridges and plateaus, as well as mountains. Across the width of the continent are oases, where towns have been built and plants grow around rare water sources.

At Guilemsi, about 50 km north of the town of Tidjikja, runs a long sandstone ridge. On rocks, boulders and the stone walls of dry riverbeds all around are ancient paintings. Some are simple handprints but others show scenes with people and animals such as horses, antelope and cattle. Around 200 km east of here is more evidence of early desert dwellers — the Tichitt culture. The remains of walls and other structures suggest that there were many Stone Age settlements in this area as long ago as 2000 BCE.

DESERT MAMMALS

1 November
Guilemsi to Oualata

Back in Tidjikja I said goodbye to my camel. I have a long way to go and I need a quicker form of transport now – a four-wheel drive. As I headed towards the small town of Oualata in south-east Mauritania, I saw herds of antelope and heard the calls of the jackals far in the distance. It got me thinking how amazing it is that animals can survive here, in one of the harshest environments on earth.

Camels

Centuries ago, Oualata was an important stop on the trans–Saharan trade route. Merchants would rest here with their camel caravans loaded up with goods to sell. Camels have long been the traditional form of transport for Saharan people and they are well suited to desert life. Their fatty humps mean they have a store of energy to burn when they can't find food in the barren desert.

Screwhorn antelope

The screwhorn antelope, or addax, is one of many types of antelope that roam the desert. It's also the largest indigenous (native) mammal in the Sahara. Sadly, the addax has been hunted almost to extinction for food and for its beautiful horns. With only 500 left in the wild, it is now critically endangered.

As I was setting up camp last night, I spotted one of the desert's best-adapted animals — a fennec fox. These small mammals spend the sweltering desert days underground and come out at night to hunt. Their large ears help them to locate their rodent prey, but importantly they also carry heat away from the fox's body to help keep it cool. Their thick fur also protects them from the sun and keeps them warm during the chilly nights.

Desert dangers

The desert may look empty, but it's actually filled with life – and not all the animals you'll find here are as cute and harmless as the fennec fox. Before you set off into the desert, find out what sort of creatures you're likely to encounter. Take a book along with you to help identify any animals or insects that may prove deadly!

CITY CULTURE

4 November
Oualata to Timbuktu

I've now crossed the border into Mali, and yesterday I finally arrived in Timbuktu, one of the few large population centres within the Sahara. I love camping in the desert, but it's great to be in a city again - to be among crowds of people and to spend a night or two in a proper bed! I've had a great day exploring this fascinating ancient city.

Women walk along the sand road past the Sankore mosque in Timbuktu.

Timbuktu

Timbuktu lies at the southern edge of the Sahara, near the River Niger. A settlement was first established here in the fifth century, and by the fifteenth century the city had become a great centre of Islamic learning and culture. It was also an important commercial hub, as people came to trade in ivory, salt and slaves. Today, the city is a World Heritage Centre, famous for its rich history and its amazing architecture.

Religion

Most people in Mali — and across the Sahara region — are Muslims, although there are also populations of Christians in some North African countries. Long ago, Timbuktu attracted many Islamic scholars. The Arabic word *Madrasah* means 'place of learning,' and there are plenty of these in Timbuktu. Three great mosques remain from the city's heyday: the Djingareyber, Sankore and Sidi Yahia. Together these make up the University of Timbuktu, which was founded more than 1,000 years ago.

Be smart, survive!

Always be aware of the dangers of the sun and the heat. Carry a water bottle with you at all times and drink from it regularly to stop yourself getting dehydrated and falling ill with heatstroke or sunstroke. Avoid travelling in the midday heat and whenever you're outside, cover yourself with sun cream and wear a hat.

I've noticed that the architecture in Mali is very unusual. A lot of buildings are made from mud-brick — sandy soil mixed with water and straw, then moulded into bricks using a rectangular frame. This ancient method of construction can be seen in the great mosques of Timbuktu as well as homes and other structures in the surrounding area. Sadly, many of the beautiful buildings in this part of the Sahara are under threat from desertification.

DROUGHT AND DESERTIFICATION

17 November
Timbuktu to Gao

I chose to get back on a camel for the journey to Gao, around 300 km from Timbuktu. As I travelled slowly along the route of the River Niger, through the southernmost part of the Sahara called the Sahel, I saw for myself the many environmental problems that this region is facing.

For the people who live in this part of the Sahara, the River Niger is a vital source of water and transportation.

Water sources

Some boundaries of the Sahara are marked by water sources, including Lake Chad in the south and the Red Sea in the east, but water is scarce in the desert itself. The River Niger and the Nile in Egypt are the only two permanent rivers in the Sahara. In some places, however, water can be found just below the surface, along stream beds that stretch out from the mountain ranges. Deeper underground there are huge layers of rock filled with water, called aquifers.

~~Sahel~~

The Sahel is the region between the arid desert parts of the Sahara and the savannas that lie to the south in sub–Saharan Africa. Human activity has caused many problems here. People have cut down trees so they can farm the land and graze livestock, but this has caused desertification and soil erosion. Global warming means that droughts are more frequent and last longer than before. This part of North Africa once supported both people and animals, but it is becoming increasingly difficult for either to survive.

Be smart, survive!

It's not easy to find water in the desert. If you need to search for a water source, climb to high ground and use a good pair of binoculars to search for valleys, as you're most likely to find water in low-lying areas. Also look out for birds and animals, which are good at finding water in even the driest environments.

Vehicles used by tourists are damaging some parts of the Sahara.

Flash floods

It's tempting to make camp in the dried creek beds known as wadis, as they can offer some protection from the wind, but this isn't a good idea! Rain may be rare in the Sahara, but sudden downpours can cause these old creek beds to fill up faster than you can get away.

13

DEADLY CREATURES

8 December
Gao to Bordji Badji Mokhtar

I've finally reached a small commune on the Mali-Algerian border. It was a long trek to get here, but it's really helped me to hone my desert survival skills. Making camp one evening, I noticed a creature scuttling across the sand and realised it was a deathstalker scorpion. Desert animals don't have to be big to be deadly!

Scorpions

The deathstalker is one of the most poisonous creatures in the desert – a sting from this large scorpion would be extremely painful at best and at worst it could kill you. These, and other species of scorpion, are well-adapted to the desert environment. They get all the liquid they need from their insect prey, and some scorpions only need to eat a couple of insects a year to survive.

Be smart, survive!

Before I climb into my sleeping bag at night, I always check it carefully for creepy-crawlies that may have sneaked inside. The same applies when getting dressed in the morning - I give my clothes a good shake before putting them on so I don't get a nasty bite from an insect that's made its bed in there!

Some snakes bury themselves just beneath the surface of the sand so you can't see them clearly.

Sidewinder snakes are common in the desert. I haven't seen a real snake yet, but I've spotted the tracks in the sand caused by their sideways slithering movement. Among the deadliest desert snakes is the horned viper, but there are many others, including huge pythons that crush their prey. In fact, nearly 100 different species of reptile make their home in the Sahara — lizards and tortoises as well as snakes.

Monitor lizards

Prehistoric-looking monitor lizards can grow to be nearly 1.5 m long! These venomous, meat-eating reptiles hunt other creatures such as rodents and insects. They can be aggressive towards humans, especially in the cold season, so it's best not to approach one if it crosses your path.

Snake checks

There are several poisonous snakes in the Sahara, including vipers and adders. To avoid getting bitten:

1 Watch where you're walking — step onto rocks and logs instead of over them.

2 Never harass a snake — many of them will attack you if they feel cornered.

3 Before you set up camp, use a stick to turn over rocks in your campsite to check no snakes are hiding underneath.

GET OUT ALIVE!!

DESERT PEOPLE

26 December
Bordj Badji Mokhtar to the Hoggar Mountains

I've ventured deeper into Algeria now, to the Hoggar Mountains. This range of peaks runs along the Tropic of Cancer, the imaginary line around the Earth halfway between the North Pole and the Equator. Here I've been able to spend some time among the Tuareg tribe - one of the highlights of my trip so far!

The Hoggar Mountains.

The Tuareg people

The Tuareg are a nomadic people who live across the southern Sahara in parts of Algeria, Niger, Mali and Libya. Like other indigenous people of the Sahara, the Tuareg are herders. They live in tents so they can move quickly and easily when the land is no longer any good for grazing. As they move around, the Tuareg visit the market places in oasis towns and villages to trade their livestock.

The Blue Men

Tuareg women do not cover their faces but Tuareg men wear veils. I was lucky enough to witness the 'first veiling' of an 18—year—old man. This takes place in a special ritual performed by a holy man called a marabout, who reads from the Qur'an as he winds the veil. The veils are made of a cloth dyed with indigo, so the Tuareg have become known as the 'Blue Men of the Desert'.

There are around 350,000 Toubou people living in the Sahara.

Be smart, survive!

It is important to keep the sand out of your eyes and keep your head cool in the glare of the sun. A long strip of muslin, around 2-3 m, can help you do both these things. Wind the muslin loosely around your neck and up over your face, covering your nose and mouth. Leaving just a slit for your eyes, keep winding it around your forehead and build it up more tightly over your head.

Other desert peoples

There are other nomadic tribes in the Sahara. The Sahrawi people live in the Western Sahara and Morocco — in fact, their name means 'from the Sahara'. The Toubou (Rock People) inhabit the Tibesti Mountains of northern Chad and southern Libya. They are divided into different clans, who live in semi—permanent settlements around water sources in the desert.

PLANT LIFE

Aïr and Ténéré Nature Reserve

The Aïr and Ténéré Nature Reserve is one of the largest national parks in Africa, covering parts of the Ténéré Desert and the Aïr Mountains. Here in this World Heritage Site I've been able to see an amazing variety of animals, including addax and other endangered antelope. The water reservoirs in the mountain valleys allow plants such as acacia and palms to flourish here.

30 December
Hoggar Mountains to Ténéré

In the bustling town of Tamanrasset I picked up a vehicle again for the next stage of my journey. It was a long drive over the border into Niger and right into the heart of the country. I've set up my camp here in a stunning nature reserve among the Aïr Mountains.

Desert plants

In general, the lack of water makes it hard for plants to grow in the desert, but some hardy species can be found in the Sahara. Acacia, palms and shrubs grow low to the ground and have long roots to reach underground water. Occasionally wild flowers can grow in the desert after a flash flood, but they are usually short-lived.

Catching water

Even in the dry desert, dew forms in the morning. If you need water, stretch out a sheet of tarpaulin on the ground or tie it between trees or even tents before you go to bed. It will catch the morning dew and provide some drinking water in times of need!

GET OUT ALIVE !!

The lonely tree

In the Sahara here in Niger there was an acacia tree known as the 'Lonely Tree of Ténéré'. It was the only tree for more than 400 km, and it provided welcome shade for merchants with their camel trains for over 300 years. It was able to grow because there was an underground well right by its roots. Sadly the tree was knocked over by a car in 1973, and all that stands in the desert here now is a memorial to the lonely acacia!

1 January
Ténéré to Bilma

I've learnt that scorpions and a lack of water aren't the only dangers the Sahara holds. As I headed deeper into the desert from Ténéré I found myself caught up in a sandstorm, which was an incredibly scary experience! It's a great relief to be lying here now under a clear sky, staring at stars that seem almost within touching distance, among the incredible sand dunes in the Erg of Bilma.

Different deserts

The name Sahara simply means 'desert' in Arabic. The Ténéré Desert is just one of many deserts within the vast Sahara, and they have several different features. Much of the El Djouf Desert in Mauritania, where I started my journey, is covered in rock salt. The Tanezrouft Desert, spanning parts of Mali, Algeria and Niger, is thousands of kilometres of barren sandstone plains.

Ergs are 'sand seas' – huge stretches of sand where nothing grows.

Ergs

I'm currently camped in the dramatic landscape of the Erg of Bilma. This is one of many ergs – vast areas of sand dunes that are constantly being shifted by the wind – in the Sahara. The loose, slippery sand makes ergs tough terrain to cross, but the dunes are brilliant for some extreme sports, including sandboarding and racing dune buggies!

Be smart, survive!

Dry winds are common in the desert. They don't all cause sandstorms, but they can still make life uncomfortable if they blow sand around. When planning your campsite, try and pitch your tent on the leeward side of sand dunes, as this will offer some protection from the winds.

Sandstorms

Desert winds can catch particles of sand or loose soil and whirl them all up off the ground to create a sandstorm. These may build into huge storms that engulf large areas. In some places the storms can take all the rich topsoil off the land, which makes it hard for plants or crops to grow. Sand can travel great distances in a storm – Saharan sands have even reached the UK!

Sandstorm danger!

GET OUT ALIVE !!

If you see a sandstorm coming, try to find some shelter, but don't keep moving when the storm strikes. Visibility can be almost zero – you may not even be able to see the sun and you'll certainly lose sight of any landmarks that might be helping you to navigate.

It's better to stay where you are until the sandstorm passes so you don't lose your way.

DESERT PEAKS

5 January
Bilma to the Tibesti Mountains

My next stop was Mount Koussi on the southern edge of the Tibesti Mountains, in Chad. I've grown used to the variety of landscapes that the Sahara has to offer, but as I stand here on the edge of the crater, looking out to the panorama beyond, I have to say this is one of the most dramatic places I've visited on my trek. The vast emptiness of it all makes me feel very small!

Saharan massifs

More than a quarter of the Saharan landscape is covered in mountains, or massifs. The impressive Atlas Mountains stretch for 2,500 km across the northern edge of the desert in Morocco and Tunisia. The mountains of the middle Sahara, where I am now, are actually the highest points of a rocky sandstone ridge that runs right across the continent. Deep gullies in the Tibesti Mountains are evidence of three great rivers that flowed here thousands of years ago, when the desert climate was more humid.

Mount Koussi

I caught a lift with a cargo truck heading out towards Mount Koussi — there aren't many roads here and it's best to travel with someone who knows the way! It's worth the detour, though. This volcano is the highest peak in the Sahara, at 3,415 m. Koussi is now extinct and no one knows for sure when it last erupted, but some experts think it may have been two million years ago! It's possible to walk to the top of Koussi to wonder at its huge crater, which is 19 km across and 1,200 m deep.

Be smart, survive!

It can get cold in the mountains at night, so I build a camp fire to keep warm. The fire also warns off any wildlife that might think about getting too close! I gather up dry sticks and pile them into a pyramid shape. If I can find dry grass I put some in the middle to help the fire light. I've kept my matches safe to make sure I can always light my camp fire!

Signal for help!

GET OUT ALIVE !!

I've brought a signalling mirror with me on my desert adventure. If I hold this up and move it around, it will catch the sun and make flashes of light that can be spotted up to 60 km away. This will help attract attention if I get lost in the mountains — or anywhere else for that matter!

OASIS LIFE

11 January
Tibesti Mountains to Kufra

Back in civilisation at last! I'm spending a few days in the Kufra oasis in Libya to rest and recharge. I'm also keen to learn what life is like in these busy settlements, which seem almost like mirages among the dry desert sands. It really is amazing how green everything is here compared to the barren mountains and desolate plains I've travelled through!

What is an oasis?

An oasis is an area of vegetation in a desert that grows up around a water source. The trees and plants are able to thrive because underground aquifers in these areas carry water close to the surface. This also means that people can dig wells to access the water, so settlements grow up around them just as they do along the banks of rivers.

Know your plants

GET OUT ALIVE!!

Many plants and trees around oases provide edible fruits that you can munch on if your food supplies are running low. Look out for olive trees, date palms and delicious figs. You might also find a doum palm, whose fruit tastes like gingerbread!

For hundreds of years, oases have been important stops for traders and travellers — and they still are today. All oases have busy, colourful marketplaces. I spent some time in the market at Kufra, watching the traders buying and selling their goods and livestock such as goats and camels. I'm surprised by the sheer numbers of people, in particular the many migrants from southern Africa, who stop off here on their journey to Europe.

Kufra oasis

The Kufra oasis in Libya is in a dip called the Kufra Basin that lies over a series of huge underground reservoirs. There are freshwater lakes here, surrounded by palm trees and other vegetation which were planted to protect the water from being polluted by sand carried by the wind. Kufra is part of a project to develop agriculture in the Sahara by running pipelines from the area to drier parts of the desert.

SAND SCULPTURES

18 January
Kufra to Qattara Depression

My amazing desert trek is nearly over. I've crossed into Egypt – the last country I'll be visiting – and I'm about to set off to explore the Qattara Depression. I took a bit of a detour to get here, though, because I'd heard about the incredible sand formations in the White Desert further south and I didn't want to miss my chance to see them!

The White Desert

So-called because of its chalk-white landscape, the White Desert is a national park and one of the Sahara's biggest tourist attractions. People come here to see the strange formations dotted across the desert landscape like giant mushrooms. These wind-formed sculptures make me feel like I'm on another planet – especially when seen by the light of my flickering camp fire.

Be smart, survive!

The glare of the sun off the desert sand can seriously damage your eyes. Symptoms can simply be your eyes feeling sore and gritty, but in extreme cases the glare can cause a temporary blindness. To prevent this, wear good sunglasses - preferably wraparounds for fuller protection. If your eyes do start to feel sore, cover them with bandages and rest them until they improve.

Qattara Depression

I've visited the highest point in the Sahara and now I'm in the lowest — the Qattara Depression, which lies 133 m below sea level just over 300 km west of Cairo. This vast, barren dip is filled with salt marshes that stretch for 300 square km across northern Egypt. They eventually meet up with the dune—covered Great Sand Sea.

Salt

The Qattara Depression isn't the only part of the Sahara where salt can be found. Trade and industry in the regions were built around the availability of salt, which was mined and sold across North Africa and beyond. Salt is still mined in the Sahara, including at the Fachi mines in Libya, and salt caravans can still be seen crossing the desert.

JOURNEY'S END

22 January
Qattara Depression to Cairo

I've arrived at my final destination - the bustling city of Cairo, capital of Egypt. However, before I catch my flight home after my epic adventure, I just have time to experience the sights, sounds and smells of this ancient settlement. As I wander through the streets, I think about how amazing it is that such a busy city thrives in the desert.

Cairo

Cairo is the largest city in the Sahara and it is absolutely packed with people. 22 million people live here, and thousands of tourists visit every month to admire the nearby pyramids and explore other remains of ancient Egyptian culture that lie further afield. The roads are filled with cars and a heavy smog hangs in the air, but despite this, Cairo is an attractive and energetic city and I enjoy wandering the streets, listening to the shouts of the market traders.

River Nile

As one of only two permanent water sources in the whole of the Sahara, the Nile is incredibly important to the ecosystem here. The river runs the full length of Egypt and eventually flows out through the Nile Delta into the Mediterranean Sea in the north. The annual flooding of the Nile makes the land on its banks very fertile, so crops can be grown.

Save the Sahara

Today, pollution and overfishing are having an environmental impact on the Nile. Seeing this makes me think about the environmental issues facing the whole Sahara region. Because the desert is so dry, people tend to crowd into the less arid regions on the edges, but this is causing huge problems. If we don't address these issues soon, the people and animals of the Sahara will be lost.

Be smart, survive!

I can't do much to stop the overpopulation in areas like the Sahel, but global warming is also causing problems there and I *can* do my bit to reduce that. When I get home I'm going to start using public transport and walking more. I'll also try to save energy around the house by switching off lights and gadgets and using energy-saving light bulbs.

GLOSSARY

aquifer A layer of underground rock that contains water.

architecture The style and design of buildings.

arid Describing somewhere that does not receive enough rain for plants to grow.

barren Describing somewhere where nothing can grow.

caravan A group of traders travelling long distances together.

climate The ususal weather conditions in a particular area.

commune A settlement where people live close together and share some possessions and amenities.

depression A large dip in the ground.

desertification The process by which farmland becomes desert.

drought A period of unexpectedly low rainfall, which causes severe water shortages.

ecosystem All the plants and animals in a particular environment.

endangered At risk of becoming extinct.

erg A large area of shifting sand dunes in a desert.

extinction The process by which a species of plant or animal dies out completely.

four-wheel drive A car where power goes to all four wheels to help it to grip the surface of the road better.

global warming The gradual increase in temperatures around the world over a period of time.

indigenous Native to an area.

indigo A tropical plant that is used to create dark blue dye.

Islamic Relating to the religion Islam, which is practised by Muslims.

leeward Towards the sheltered side (downwind).

livestock Farm animals that are raised for meat or trade.

massif A compact group of mountains.

memorial Something that is put up so people will remember a person, thing or event.

migrants People who move to another country to live.

nomadic Describing people who move around rather than living in one place.

plateau A large area of high, level ground.

reptile A cold-blooded animal that lays eggs.

sandstone A type of red or brown rock made of sand or quartz.

savanna A large grassy area where only a few trees grow.

scholar Someone who studies a particular subject.

soil erosion The process by which the top layer of soil is washed away by water or blown away by the wind.

tarpaulin Heavy-duty waterproof cloth.

INDEX & FURTHER INFORMATION

Books

Deserts (Amazing Habitats) by Leon Gray (Franklin Watts, 2014)
Deserts (Geographywise) by Leon Gray (Wayland, 2014)
The Sahara Desert (Deserts Around the World) by Molly Aloian (Crabtree Publishing, 2012)

Websites

http://geography.howstuffworks.com/africa/the-sahara-desert.htm
http://www.livescience.com/23140-sahara-desert.html
http://www.sciencekids.co.nz/sciencefacts/earth/desert.html

TRAVELLING
WILD
TPB09-5

OTHER TITLES IN THE TRAVELLING WILD SERIES

9780750285841

9780750298612

9780750298643

9780750298650

9780750283052

9780750283236

9780750283243

9780750283250